Spirited and searching poems by an acclaimed poet, novelist, essayist who is also one of Japan's most innovative businessmen: Tsujii Takashi is the pen name of Tsutsumi Seiji, founder of a group that includes the Inter-Continental Hotel chain and Seibu Department Stores.

In Japan he has received a number of literary prizes; France has named him an *Officier de l'Ordre de la Légion d'Honneur;* Austria has awarded him the Commander's Cross 1st Class for *Services to the Republic of Austria* in the area of culture.

His book *A Spring Like Any Other*, awarded the Taiko Hirabayashi Prize, is available from Kodansha International.

Japanese names are given in the traditional order, family name first.

Asian Poetry in Translation: Japan

Editor, Thomas Fitzsimmons

#1 *Devil's Wind: A Thousand Steps* by Yoshimasu Gozo
#2 *Sun, Sand and Wind* by Shozu Ben
#3 *A String Around Autumn: Selected Poems 1952-1980* by Ooka Makoto
#4 *Treelike: The Poetry of Kinoshita Yuji* — Japan-US Friendship Commission Translation Prize
#5 *Dead Languages: Selected Poems 1946-1984* by Tamura Ryuichi
#6 *Celebration in Darkness: Selected Poems of Yoshioka Minoru & Strangers' Sky: Selected Poems of Iijima Koichi*
#7 *A Play of Mirrors: Eight Major Poets of Modern Japan*, anthology
#8 *A Thousand Steps . . . and More: Selected Poems and Prose 1964-1984* by Yoshimasu Gozo
#9 *Demented Flute: Selected Poems 1967-1986* by Sasaki Mikiro
#10 *I Am Alive: The Tanka Poems of Goto Miyoko*
#11 *Moonstone Woman: Selected Poems and Prose* by Tada Chimako
#12 *Self-Righting Lamp: Selected Poems* by Maruyama Kaoru
#13 *Mt. Fuji: Selected Poems 1943-1986* by Kusano Shinpei
#14 *62 Sonnets and Definitions* by Tanikawa Shuntaro
#15 *The New Poetry of Japan: the 70s and 80s*, anthology
#16 *Disappearance of the Butterfly*, by Tsujii Takashi

Supported by the National Endowment for the Arts, the Japan-US Friendship Commission, Oakland University (MI), University of Michigan Center for Japanese Studies, the Saison Cultural Foundation (Japan), the University of Sydney (Australia), and UNESCO.

DISAPPEARANCE OF THE BUTTERFLY

Asian Poetry in Translation: Japan #16

DISAPPEARANCE OF THE BUTTERFLY

Tsujii Takashi

Translated by
Robert Brady &
Susanne Akemi Wegmüller

Preface by Awazu Norio

KATYDID BOOKS SANTA FE

KATYDID BOOKS
1 Balsa Rd., Santa Fe, New Mexico 87505

Distributed by **University of Hawaii Press**
2840 Kolowalu St., Honolulu, HI 96822
FAX: (808) 988 6042

Produced by KT DID Productions.

Printed and bound in the United States of America on acid free paper.

First edition

Library of Congress Cataloging in Publication Data

Tsujii, Takashi
[Poems. Selections. English]
Disappearance of the Butterfly / by Tsujii Takashi ; translated by Robert Brady and Wegmüller Akemi.
p. cm. — (Asian Poetry in Translation. Japan ; #16)
Translated from various books in Japanese.
ISBN 0-942668-43-X : $24.95 — ISBN 0-942668-44-8 : $12.95
1. Tsujii, Takashi—Translations into English. I. Brady, Robert. 1940- . II. Wegmüller, Akami. III. Title. IV. Series.
PL839.S879A23 1994
895.6′15—dc20 94-9980
CIP

DISAPPEARANCE OF THE BUTTERFLY

Introduction

by Awazu Norio

Dark, chaotic sentiments roiling, their outlet blocked shut. A material sense founded on a rough touch. An almost scorching pursuit of ideals. Social conscience alloyed with piercing criticism. A dogged resolve to achieve precise form. All these diverse elements coexist in Tsujii Takashi. Of course, they do not come together naturally. They are in dangerous contradiction and opposition to each other, sometimes even giving rise to mutual negation. However, the attempt to avoid this result by holding these elements ambiguously within oneself, never examining them thoroughly, can lead to something much more dangerous: autointoxication.

In trying to prevent this outcome, most people would probably locate the one element most essential to themselves, and taking it as nucleus, position the other elements in relativity around it. Tsujii Takashi, however, did not take that approach. Selecting the contradictory elements within himself, he pushed each one forward, creating a place in imagination where they could come together in vivid correspondence. He had no choice: each of his diverse self-elements was inextricably bonded to a profound part of his life.

In Tsujii Takashi's case, moreover, these profound parts of his life were not dwelling naturally inside him as, for example, childhood memories. His complex personal history compelled him to hold deep doubts as to the meaning of his own existence. Also, the leftist political movement to which he dedicated himself after the war, and its frustrations, carved in him a bitter distrust of politics and people, and of himself. Consequently, while these profound parts of his life inform the core of his being, they cannot exist within him as anything but time bombs, capable of their own negation. In this sense, Tsujii Takashi was forced to set out from a place wholly deprived of the potential for direct action.

Naturally, his poetry has always borne these heavy themes and painful conditions. Japanese poetry after the war was first forged by the poets of the *Arachi* (Wasteland) and *Rettou* (Archipelago) movements. The *Arachi* poets remained in the modernist tradition of the prewar years but with a critical attitude tried to go beyond it, while the *Rettou* poets were rooted in the leftist poetry of the prewar years but tried to conquer simple politicism in favor of introducing a new strategy-consciousness. One may say that Tsujii Takashi, coming one generation after these poets, was deeply influenced by both schools, but he melded them together, within the lack of direct action that is his condition, in order to realize his own unique voice.

This condition compelled him to find complex devices for his poetry, and it is interesting that he uses metaphor as his strongest weapon in this endeavor. Naturally, in Tsujii Takashi's case metaphor is not merely a form of rhetoric; rather, it corresponds directly to the lack of direct action which is the condition of his life.

By 1961, when he published *Ihoujin* (*Strangers*), his second collection of poems after *Futashikana Asa* (*An Uncertain Morning*), his poetry already bore the stamp of his own unmistakable style. While "made one person unhappy / two people unhappy / on the path I have walked lies / my corpse" (from "Arrogance") is certainly very poignant, this poignancy is matched by a glimpse of raw immediacy. Later, however, he would move closer to an overall immediacy which would also be more metaphorical, thus giving his metaphors more complex expression and freedom.

This characteristic of his poetry was almost garishly manifested in his 1978 collection, *Hako Matawa Shingou eno Koshitsu* (*Clinging to Boxes and Signals*). Taking as his subject such objects as a toothbrush, broom, teakettle, spoon, umbrella, and bicycle his style was reminiscent of Francis Ponge; however, through his concentration on these everyday objects, Tsujii Takashi's imagination is even more varied than Ponge's in his treatment. While the connection between his concentration on these objects and his imaginative flights can be somewhat suffocating at times, we may say that through subjection to that danger, Tsujii Takashi asserted his own essential direction.

In his 1985 collection, *Tatoete Setsugekka* (*For Example, Snow, Moon, Flowers*), his subjects comprised such flowers as the narcissus, violet, hydrangea and mountain lily. In his 1987 collection, *Tori Mushi Sakana no Me ni Namida*, he turned to the woodpecker, seagull, grasshopper, fish and other creatures. This transition from inanimate objects to flowers and wildlife was probably Tsujii's way of overcoming that sense of suffocation, and injecting the freedom of nature into his poetry. As a result, his metaphors as well were released from the spell of objectification and began to exhibit a multilayered freedom of movement, at the same time giving rise to a sort of narrative power.

In his 1989 collection, *Younaki Hitono* (*Man of No Use*), Tsujii Takashi's subjects were people such as a swimming person, a playing person, a person passing, a woman printing, a woman writing in her journal and a running man. This progression, from tools to flowers, flowers to creatures, creatures to humans beings, was by no means simply aiming for novelty. Rather, I should say it was an extremely methodical reflection of the maturation and deepening of his metaphorical method. In this collection, the poet did not concentrate his gaze in a particularly conscious fashion on anything; rather, he opened his eyes and spirit naturally to the world at large. By doing so, he was able to create for himself a standpoint from which the whole of his imagination could move with miraculous spontaneity. Metaphor had become a mirror reflecting the entire world.

This was realized brilliantly in "Man Running," for example. However, in his 1992 work, *Gunjou, Waga Mokushi* (*Ultramarine, My Revelation*) Tsujii's world expands further, from one point in the present to the contemporary history of an era. Skillfully integrating the techniques and framework of T.S. Eliot's "The Wasteland," and combining these aspects with the metaphorical method he had cultivated over the years, Tsujii Takashi forged an amazing ability to see through and illuminate Japan in the present age.

Bicycle

(On seeing a bicycle at the Louisiana Museum)

Handlebars grasped
the blood flowed toward the bicycle
Settled onto the saddle
the spirit raced off to an aimless destination

So on the late afternoon beach
as it fell into darkness
houses in the sun faded away
and walls the fragrance of dry grass crumbled

The boy's shadow was surprisingly indistinct

In a space that once was free as a blue fish
a flower called cosmos blooms
honeybees and butterflies are flittering
but I can't imagine there'd be light or wind

Seagulls flew in from the sea
called once then traced gentle arcs
and crabs peered at the sea from between the rocks
but this is unrelated to who I am now
Even less can the bicycle wheels, endlessly turning
be explained with formal logic

Excessiveness is not permitted
the chain was there to mesh with the gears, yet
now each asserted its own identity

an exquisite and reluctant complex

Undulating like snakes
secretly yearning for a place where passion and precept conjoin
the spokes, once bearers of love
are fundamental laws of geometry
sectioning the four directions

The consequence of function as measure
is the reduction of function to its parts
Therefore rolling the bicycle out of the shed of memory
doesn't mean I can mount my life on it
The body that should ride is already part of the splendid
  mechanism
so eyes of family hatred fall upon it

No matter how hard you pedal
you can't reach eternal being

This knowledge makes dreaming impossible
a sacrilege in fact

In this forsaken transmigration
the only action remaining is to grope
we can no longer see the way
And then strangely
the bicycle, regaining kingly dignity
and becoming the embodiment of other nations' tools
began to move within its cage of glass
Just when I'd surrendered to bereavement
and should've flung black crepe upon it
somehow it seems the crepe has only fallen on my eyes
Assuming the posture of bicycle rider
lightly clenched fists, forward crouch

I realized: this is the posture for space travel
and the pose we use to float through the world

Unfathomable sadness
an arrow of malignant light streaking toward the wall
transfixed me

A quiet afternoon in the museum in Copenhagen
the bicycle, now an oblivion-affirming object
travels on

Comb

Dawn does not break from a comb
night simply grows deeper
The pink comb floating in the clam-colored sky
resembles the lips of a soothsayer
but does not announce daybreak
Dissonance   spreading to the horizon and filled with fertile
  wilderness
How good it feels
Vomit-soured breath   the satiation of artificial scents
is there anything one can give
to someone setting out   to avoid these   seeking to dry out
Not a comb of plastic
but a tower standing still
in the monsoon region of Toyoashibara
        the Land of Abundant Rice
where soot and smoke hover
Around it   the tenacity of swarming flies
Humanness   the source of shamelessness
    is the mother of civilization
Rolling billows of waves   Hiroshige or Kuniyoshi
Thinking I should look deeply into myself as well
    I stretch out my hand
and see in the flood of TV commercials the overlapping
  images of
a hand pushing open a door
a hand made to display its ring
a hand   fingertips white from clutching a bottle tight
a hand so tired its veins stand out
hands so close I could almost touch them   but I can't

I see countless hands
Even if I poise myself thinking
    What I need now
    is a fine-tooth comb to remove the grime
The impurity of my hands will not be cleansed day will not dawn
Even if I recall that day breaks from within one's breast
There the shadow of a woman sinking as she writhes in pain
is throwing a comb into the land of the dead
Large ravens cawing thrice in ill omen and flying away
The wind is full of spells to ward off evil
Since when were the shrieks of Osore-zan[1]
introduced in Kiyushoren[2] and the *Guide Bleu*
even today experts continue their commentary
Are combs of mother-of-pearl gilt-lacquer coral
the fat of contentment or the heavy make-up of the System
The combs and dolls brought to the wedding
  by a bride untouched in heart
  "Before long she lay upon her sick-bed took leave of the world
  and around the princess's pillow each night the doll's hair grew longer."
At this story of the princess who died so young
steel H-beams blacken completely with gathered soot
and the castle walls of Asia lengthen at the crystallization of karmic tales
stone walls pregnant with moisture
where in rainy season an exquisite moss grows
Through the long rainy spell that does not distinguish night from day
a man trudges away hoping to dry out
A kiss thrown at his retreating figure Does it do the trick
not a comb
At least the ivory tower has no relation

A slight education is at once washed away by rain
behaving gravely is therefore ineffective
So I criticize in full vexation
and give up waiting for dawn
It's like waiting a hundred years for the Yellow River to clear
and now I make plans to set off in my Mustang
Can the 150 horsepower twin carburetors
sever the viscosity of history
Providing beverages is the task of vending machines
One box of Kleenex
And Seven Stars cigarettes are enough
All I need in addition are a few cassette tapes
Peterson's "Night Train" Monk
Miyako Harumi and I'm happy
I don't need a comb
There is nothing that is certain
All I'm certain of
is that this comb is made of plastic
so I won't chant any spells or recite any prayers
I will seek combs of boxwood rosewood whalebone
Should this be called contentment
to have something to look for
At any rate dawn does not break from a comb
Morning will likely begin once more with negation

---

[1] Osore-zan: A sacred mountain in Aomori, literally "Fear Mountain" where mediums call the dead, who can be heard answering.

[2] Kiyushoren: An encyclopedia of sorts concerning Edo period customs, practices, entertainments.

Cosmos

Bruised flower petals flying in the anticipated sky
of a gentle sailor smiling despite
being shut up in a box
Cosmos petals go scattering
in the obscure light flooding the deep blue
of fragrant flesh
When willy-nilly drawn into hell
transcending the proper order of all things
like a seagull at the end of its journey
he closes his eyes and leans back
against the receding memories of a voyage at sea
a translucent melody
rolls away riding the harmony of the waves
The clouds that continue their explosions
at the edge of the splendrous Earth
    do they still give bloom to thunderclaps
Although it cannot be seen
far beyond the horizon
is a sense that colors are bursting in the millennium
The echoes of ceaselessly roaring artillery
cannons more cannons
The Earth's axis is pitching
so trying harder to believe
taunting full-force
this self-relinquishment that resembles stupidity
he is satisfied that what is correct has been proven
The gaunt jealous inquisitors
become a warm wind and run along the deck

singing the praises of intellect
Once they too loved the sea and flowers
but the compass stays carefully hidden away
The sailor faces the stuffed effigy of perished faith
and writes "today my mother died"
In a time without end
a forgotten ballad is heard
from southern islands where aboriginals live
He takes out a hard nut
from the hold as the ship retraces the meridian
enduring the stubborn fatuity
of the imprecision inherent in all words
and placing this round artifact of nostalgia on his palm
gazes at it in a boundless brightness
bit by bit the blue of the sea grows deeper
The creaking of the box
is hope attempting to fly away
because the ship has lost balance and listed
Struggling to escape the arms that clutch it tight
and take wing
it sinks the plummet descends
Within unfathomable illusions
the cosmos become birds
Holding up the flock of pink flowers
are their tremulous stems
the sunset glow that scorches thought
a hushed heaviness and
a repetition that cannot be named

The Crumbled Man

(For Francis Bacon)

The man crumbled
not because he worried too much
on the contrary with never a doubt
he earnestly concentrated his consciousness
tensed his muscles and worked
like a falcon intent upon its prey
Long chains of hours challenging work objectives
And yet for some reason he tired
So much as not even to notice he'd begun to crumble
Seating himself in a chair he folds his arms and thinks
puts one leg across the other
moves hands to hold up his sinking chin
nurses his melting shoulders
Lowering his head he looks for his lost shadow
become a hole in the floor with neither eyes nor nose
Why Where How
What has changed Don't ask me such things
Since I wouldn't know
about the world
When it comes to people though leave it to me
"Abilities background habits school records sports at
which they
excel how much liquor they drink how often they smoke
performance at work relations with their friends
family members hobbies right- or left-handed" etc. etc.
I input it all to the host computer
The man regains his self-confidence

becomes a bit sleepy   closes his eyes
Somewhere   a school bell is sounding the start of class
"Edwards"   calls a teacher
The man recalls that yellow dandelions were blooming
at the foot of the bridge that spanned the dried-up river
As he shifts
he notices his feet are stuck together   won't come apart
nose   mouth   even the corners of his eyes have begun to
 crumble
The man watches himself drooping
Thinks   I'll input this to my computer as well
it's new data   and gloats

Disappearance of the Butterfly

The stars were unusually bright toward dawn
because last night the butterfly died
Dreams of marble seen in dim light
come gleaming upon firm smooth skin
Closing my eyes at thoughts transparently pale crimson
I tenderly kiss the demons of history
and burn an illusory incense
The fossils burned
to fumigate the pleasures of this life
  are unexpectedly cold
When the veil and the wind played together
and the butterfly
descending the stairway of eternity toward the rooftop garden
singing the transience of this world
became musical notes of the unconscious
all things certain were weakened
The cherry blossoms and chrysanthemums were blooming in
  yesterday's skies
so flying to a past where it could shine
it found no landscape there
Only human skins rolled into belts of efficiency
branding themselves with the marks of madness   loyalty
  and filial piety
were bobbing up and down in hours long past
The mandarin duck   having promptly given up flight
now stands stuffed   facing the globe
in a parlor where curtains flutter
serenely pondering the tragedy of modern times

Just then faint feelings of guilt wafted up
without knowing their owner became a trailing spring haze
and from inside it the butterfly was born
The beauties of nature were bleached
and acidic rain fell several times
but the butterfly did not die
In time the sun comes out birds chirp
and a little girl on a bicycle rides away
cheerfully waving an arm
without any sense of guilt
Everything is so very natural
that Zarathustra completely lost heart
and stopped speaking
The butterfly laboriously crosses
not the Tatar Strait
but the Sea of Fertility created by the "soulless engineer"
High low
resembling a lyric
that trembles on a barbed-wire staff
but what is heard is neither love song
nor lullaby
and the derangement grows quietly deeper
Through the space of imagination the butterfly flies on
The flow of time has neither purpose nor feeling
so neither hate nor the effort to endure embarrassment has
any effect
History is always salty like a dried-up lake
and dreams alone change the time and space of cruelty
to ultramarine
so even if light radiates in serenity
and flower petals scatter on the precipice
even if the chrysanthemums in the rooftop garden stand
in uniformed rows
the butterfly is untouched does not draw near

Passing through a room of *fin-de-siecle* design
a breeze is stirring
For the entire world to become a palace
all the marble
had to be packed in wrappings of resignation
but fortunately there was an eccentric
so the yellow ripening never occurred
and the butterfly was able to cross
after passing the danger of a fall
instead of becoming a heavenly body stopped in orbit
set on the scales at the window ledge
it is neither conscience nor love nor the laws of economic
  development
and the butterfly's eyelashes grow heavy
at sight of nightingales in plum trees dew on bush clover
because Venus has just risen at the edge of temptation
dripping water from hair and fingertips
The butterfly daydreaming among pistils and stamens
missed its chance to fly away
Surrendering its idea of sliding into history
because it was deep in conversation with the tapir[1]
  fat from devouring philosophy
the butterfly drifts toward the sunset
over the twenty-four hours of a sanctuary
The pregnant marble holds its silence
but what will bloom in time is not a violet but the flower
 of desire
At this prediction the stone turns pale crimson
The butterly must have passed over it
Like a fish fertilizing eggs
it lurched trailing shrieks behind it
and what happened to it after that nobody knows
The veil flutters in the wind turns over

This morning at dawn
an unusually large rainbow spanned the sky

---

[1] In this case, a mythical Chinese beast with elephant-like trunk, rhinoceros-like eyes, cow-like tail and bear-like body, that eats the nightmares of humans.

Fireflies

The light of fireflies   because of the dark
is handy for examining wounds
Glimmering faintly   resisting the wind
like masthead lamps inside the memory
after treasure-seeking steamer-galleons have sunk
they make hydrangeas bloom
The flowers flicker in the rain
The world moves slowly into a large urn
Battles certain to end in defeat
portray the vision of the millennium
and desertion begets an ostentatious feast
Then   flying on the underside of the soul
fireflies   from the distant Milky Way
In silence
they collide with the walls of our ephemeral world
There is no way to escape
Hanging in the breast of a man meditating one hundred
  years
the body of a spy
floating on the dimly lit horizon
the site of execution is not marked on the map
There   even now
countless flocks of sheep avalanche
and a caravan travels a narrow winding path   carrying arms

Like a bell swaying in the breeze
wisdom plays with wineskin
When calculation eventually

approaches a faint   wasted smile
one more firefly is born
On the rim of the empty urn
with humble merchant forebears
with a man who counted coins
in humble quantities   alone
always late at night
for a father
with a woman who dampened the seams of her darning
with tears of sorrow
for a mother
firefly leans a ladder against the urn
and descends with firm steps   rung by rung
Defying the interrogation of the Grand Inquisitor
and flattering himself that he bears the glory to create an era
he taps out a rhythm
yearns for still unsullied desire
licks the world's scars meaningfully
making sport of tenderness
That's why
the firefly intensifies his glow at each nightfall
in time symbolizing dead souls
Vacantly he begins to flit about
The malice of Minamoto Yorimasa[1]   become modern
at this time   gathers in Uji and commences battle
but alas   the arsenal remains dormant
and the birds of passage promptly feign ignorance and vanish
melting into the darkness to fabricate alibis
The slender moon declined
wrapped in mist   like a ghost
and lost its razor edge
A long journey
after billions of light years
following a straight way

flying the path of love to Almighty God
and there beginning a charming tale —
not a violet but an unheavy light
perhaps the diffused reflection
of rust that opened holes in the night
It's not finely wrought mother-of-pearl
so you don't need eyes to see it or words
just feeling it is enough
Trying to crawl up from the bottom of the urn
every advance in this creeping that resembles futile labor
turns to the seeds of a split pomegranate
For the sake of mutual redemption
senselessly hurling coins at each other
gloomily sounding resounding echoes
The fireflies seeking sweet water
begin to move as one against the dark flow
flying without the sound of wings
barely flying
they head toward the tombstones of the present
nebulously making of themselves the Milky Way

---

[1]Minamoto Yorimasa (1106 -80) samurai ally of the Taira clan who committed suicide after noble defeat against tremendous odds in the Battle of Uji bridge.

Hydrangea

Lost blue sky
floating in the dull light   the shape of small worlds
hydrangeas in full bloom
ebb and flow inside memory   colors fade
indiscernibly   soundlessly deepen
apparently tenuous
because the wind is uncertain
Passing showers   white in the shade of trees
In sorrow expanding with no aim in mind
                                        the flower puts on rouge
Once   to endure was to wait
Divining the position of the sun
attempting to find warmth
in the courses of birds that even now
                                        should be flying in dark clouds
and tightly grasping scars grown indistinct
self-assurance   about to crumble
strays into the frontier of fog
Holding up the low-hanging sky
is a song for survival
a phalanx of pointed shoots
With no words against dissension
the masquerade ball disappears into unblinking time
The ascending scale falters
and shadows turn pale
In a stillness resembling the fate
of acquiescence
droplets trickle

toward the depths of being
Since brightness is nowhere to be seen
the hydrangea dresses up and sways
white to purple   eventually red
Regrets   too many to comprehend   rain down
Suppressing the lonesome expression that struggles to
  appear
and smiling
is the wisdom of knowing wasted effort
Trying to bury expectations with one's own hand
before the ruin that eventually visits
The weak betrayal   of gentleness

Man of No Use

Man of no use loses form
man of no use becomes water

Man of no use is of little weight
man of no use becomes   wind   cloud   sound

Man of no use forgets
Man of no use becomes shadow

Sound has vibrations
that speed across flourishing wasteland
    Do not look for meaning
Somewhere someone is carving stone
the chisel-sound flies across distance
     becomes a disheveled bird

Man of no use   blown by the wind
becomes a lingering shadow
At the foot of the bridge at the edge of town
tears   when did they spill over
become black-headed gulls
and fly among rubbish and dust

Water swirls into a whirlpool
columns of bubbles rise from the depths
twirl themselves pout and vanish
   (The one we envision is there   not there)
On the water's surface appears the face of a corpse

The head of the woman he left behind tilts
  sways distorting slightly
Beyond youths for whom time is lost
move in a herd
  like water plants that yield to mourning
The people wither
and are swept far away beneath the bridge
as far as vision goes
Time passes

Obstinate soldiers observing ancient rules
  went down drowning gasping for air
  between the waves swept by the wind
  they sank without voice
  on that day no sun no trembling leaves
Only the gods of betrayal escaped with their lives
On the back streets many stone monuments proclaiming
  something

Man of no use does not look back
passes houses lit by the evening sun
Alphabets dance in his breast
The town blazes The sky blazes
The river sends forth flames
Sadness seduces the light like a woman's hair
In the pale depths a song weeps
denying the winds of erosion

Man of no use becomes wind
changes places with stone monuments
Still uncertain of where he's going
he drapes himself with the landscape
losing heaviness
  Clouds are bearing up malice and worship

    Does lyricism become wings
    or does it become the delicate petals of flowers
    that scatter on the breeze

In a playground unseen   children are singing
their voices become limpidly translucent
the circle becomes a crane

Man of no use
looks up at the blinding verge of time
he poles through the weariness
       of livelihood sodden
         among computers and work stations
           of the destination of the staff of life
and remembers days that leaped into mid-air

Nostalgia for a castle shaped of will
The dignity of this illusory fortress
What is it that echoes in the evening sky
It isn't morning so
the buzzing must be of insects
ephemerally soaring
wings aquiver with song
slowly disappearing into the depths

Man of no use
thought he'd like to take a journey
his desire to roam
all the stronger for not coming true

As he leans against the bridge
the noise   like the flash that destroyed soldiers in the past
shoots through the sky where only a slight glow remains
  floating

The wind has a forgiving spirit
separating roadside trees and arching lights
it lays down language
The letters on the monuments have worn away
  Do not search for what is gone

Somewhere sounds of voices arguing
In the twilight clay blossoms

Man of no use stands upright
Imitating a gossamer-winged mayfly
he prepares to take wing from the foot of the bridge
the ferryman appears on the water and calls
(Hurry Get into the boat Day is done)

Man Running

1

The running man is healthy
most of all because he's satisfied with himself
Knowing there's no heaven in this world
he shows consideration
puts a smile on his face
and starts his race from beneath the cherry tree
his company's logo on his forehead
Mt. Fuji pictured in his mind
but since his sidearms don't belong in peacetime
he got rid of them long ago
and while he was at it   art as well
So   much lighter
he passed one milestone after another
Running through still sleeping neighborhoods
if he passes a newsboy
he just nods
sometimes he says "Howdy"
he gets no answer of course   but it doesn't matter
a second later   they're far apart
Social relations should be kept simple
don't meddle in other people's lives
Even robots have human rights
but in return are spied upon
Reporters number some fifty thousand
so make some noise   whoop it up
but around the neighborhood   better keep quiet
"What does your next-door neighbor do"

Likes to write haiku in his spare time
"So devoted to his family
and his wife so gentle and soft-spoken"
You never know when you might get involved in some
  incident
must have the neighbors speak well of you
"Preparation is all" as they say
One never knows when the bomb will go off
so surely
yet uncertainly
the town continues crumbling around the running man
But no one is surprised or panicky
They don't even seem to think it's strange
so perhaps the ruin
is not advancing
The present the future
it's smarter not to think about them so much
Seriousness is the worst thing for one's health and for
  success
and isn't even fashionable anymore
In the old days
he would have burned all his philosophy books
but no need to worry
he can leave them to the hand of an unseen God[1]
they won't get in the way of his running
There are no spectators
so he can give himself full concentration
The man feels a stirring excitement unseemly at his age
becomes a little uneasy as well
That's why he should just keep running

yesterday and again today
breathlessly
out of the fog

a white dog with floppy ears is coming after him

2

The running man has no friends
"Everybody dies alone" goes the old refrain
But it's not as if he's dead
On the other hand he isn't really alive
Since he doesn't want to become pampas grass[2]
since he doesn't want to be arrested
don't ask him for whom for what in rapid fire
the man doesn't know either
Or maybe he's already caught
by the castle by rules and regulations
Speaking of which he just passed a large gate
the gatekeeper was sitting down
but that was a device we call a promise
Is he running now on the inside
Or is it the outside
It is written that one should do one's utmost
to "enter in at the strait gate"[3]
so there must be something inside if you do
Flowers stars maybe heaven
"Going is easy but coming back is scary"[4]
so the man looks at the gate from the corner of his eye
and crosses the bridge
Looking down
at the clear river of ancient times
dirty in the present
run dry in the future
he listens to his footsteps echo on the railing
The upper regions are clear they say
but the fog is thick

so the sun rises like a backdrop
and the scene is somehow stage-like
He realizes the gate was also part of the set
All those hurdles he cleared
in dead earnest every time
O beautiful time of youth
when he had his bottom smacked and the whip upon him
all the many gates he passed through
It started then
his ceaseless running
avoiding gates at all costs
And he was made section head before anyone else
soon after department manager Heave
by and by he'll be head of the division Heave ho
and after that and after that Yo heave ho
With all this his self-satisfaction is inevitable
(but there's still a long way to go)
The running man is carrying an important message
a divine oracle instructions from the managing director
Health-consciousness is catching on
so tying on a chrysanthemum-patterned headband
with his wife's encouragement "Have a good run
and be careful dear"
he left the house
Marriage is another obstacle race
he ruminates as he waits for the light to change
Crossroads are important in life just don't cross too early
This sense of timing is surely the key to success
the guardian angel of order he thinks as he runs in place
Then realizes this came from a colleague's speech
at a celebration party
That he hasn't a single original thought
is the man's pride the symbol of his daily rising status
In this age everything is ready-made

so the man took off on this a new morning
same as all mornings

Inside the house his lovely wife is running too
it's good to be slim
good for beauty and good for sex
So matching her breathing to the man's
and supervising the children's homework
she turns to the wall to look in a slightly weary rhythm
at the picture frame of her youth
that she'd departed without seeing through
Since she knows no adventure besides having affairs
if she makes sure that fancy alone is free
all that remains of Narcissus is a yellow flower
When she ventures to look at herself in the water
she sees her husband running through fog
Why did a sudden feeling of contempt move her then
She thinks what if her husband died
(I wonder if I still have some youth left in me)
Turning back to the real mirror she smiles faintly
knowing just how Madame Bovary felt
she raises her pumping thighs higher

Just at that time the running man passes a traveler
in sedge hat and straw poncho[5]
trudging along seeking the beauties of nature
some sort of shadow maybe at his side
It bothers the man
    was it a smell perhaps the smell of history
But he can't very well slacken his brisk pace
he has an important task after all
The stamina to keep on running
    even beyond the Japanese archipelago
is just in order to guard happiness

(Good shopping means family bliss)[6]
to stay healthy
until the day his loans are paid in full
far away from elegance grace simplicity
The spirit of seclusion from an imperfect world
and dreams of floating free in the sea
are brushed off
gallantly and also unconsciously
by shaking his head shaking his body

trying not to hear
the footsteps of his pursuer the white dog
pat pat pat pat pat pat pat pat
who comes after him wherever he goes

3

Into his dreams
into the darkness of his bright future
even into his commuter train
the white dog comes running — whose reincarnation?
His feudal lord or proxy bailiff
but wait the castle was supposed to have sunk
Discrimination and inequality are now prohibited
even wild beasts are protected
to say nothing of domestic animals[7]
so there's no reason for him to be pursued
and yet unmistakably footsteps are approaching
Mingled with drops of invisible rain
like a voice calling from far away
the man remembers the woman's whisper
"Run away with me
somewhere where no one will follow"

Knowing there is no promised land
and yet appealing to him this way
she seemed to him so sweet
that he let himself join her in dreaming
Why did he become afraid   back then
The running man turns the corner at the tobacco shop
sees the main gate of another temple before him and thinks
what is permitted is flight from flight
in step with the movement of running
His student days when he pondered life —
but more than philosophy he enjoyed music
he joined a choir and sang hallelujah
when they hit a harmony it was as though the world expanded
and his body swayed too to the beat of rock n' roll
And his romance with the soprano   now his wife —
they say not even one revolution went unbetrayed
Before long the man considered escape with the woman
(There sure are many ways of running)
Running off   running out   runnning late
Heading for the Millennium and burning out
Staggering toward Nirvana
The parade for the construction of a shining village
The responsibility the man is bearing — what is it for
Who ordered it
No longer sure where he should deliver it
he just runs at a steady speed
Ten years as if it were a day   with untiring perseverance
aiming for the Seniority and Diligence Awards
This feeling that his hair is being pulled back
when he turns with the road
this sense that his flesh   heavy like *mochi*
is moving away from his backbone
is it because the temple gate he saw a while back
is calling him

His birthplace hasn't existed for him for a long time now
so let's banish nostalgia   ignore tradition
feeling himself for once   an athlete representing
the modern age
the man straightens his posture
Proud feelings flow into his lungs
Names and quantities of exported products
are being fed ceaselessly into computers
From between the gaps in that sound
echoes — strangely enough — a temple bell
tolling the strains of the vanity of all things
In the sky   where darkness remains
lotus flowers bloom   one after another
Spring and summer have become one
thanks to biotechnology
It's the dawn of a splendid mixed culture
A streak of light pierces the neighborhood
and the mice nimbly hide in their holes
Rubbish is heaped at housefronts here and there
The blue car with the gingko-leaf mark isn't here yet
so there isn't even that to cut off his route

But the white dog follows behind him
A hunting dog   judging from his face
His legs   slender like a cat's   chase his prey
with unvarying speed
through the gradually expanding sounds
he follows behind   passing the still sleeping houses

4

The man spits onto the guardrail
Looking up at the senselessly blinking traffic light

he sends a greeting to the "Let's keep our neighborhood clean"
of the trash receptacles donated by the Boys Club and
women's group
Surveying the area he exchanges glances
with the show windows
and wonders if artificial flowers have dreams too
At night men and women are intimate under roofs
the world over
Morning comes men the world over go running moodily
and in due time hurry silently to work
Even so he's satisfied with himself
(so no danger in free-association)
the man runs harder in place
and from deep within this gesture
confirming his place in the majority
he hears an out-of-place song
"Life is dark and death is dark"[8]
The light changes
The running man crosses the crosswalk respectably
The inconvenience of a bright affluent neighborhood
is that too many rules envelop it
There is no way to escape
but knowing if he doesn't escape the dog will get him
he thinks just until I see this responsibility through
When he tries to recall what documents he was to hand
to whom
he feels as though he's forgotten something important
It was all so clear when he was a boy —
Koshien[9] inventor government minister
He used to walk under the silk trees
pretending he was a movie star
and race across fields where sunflowers bloomed
as far as the eye could see
He used to look at fallen leaves and cry like a violin

Glancing at a car that had spent the night on the street
the man changes course and heads for the park
He remembers that last night   he dreamed he visited
                                        the rose garden of Heaven
the gatekeeper who pressed him for his admission fee
the flood of flowers he could only sense
the sight of himself waking to gaze blankly upon
                                                the disorderly room
so vivid it scarcely seems himself
so that was part of the dream too
because he had gotten up to go to work
Looking out the bus window he had seen the faded flags
                                        of faraway countries
fluttering in the wind stirred by passing cars
On the windows of the oval building opposite
a poster for consumer credit   "Vacancy"
and "Word processing" and "Copies made here"
The Chinese restaurant is still asleep
Was there such a thing as glory of the flag . . .
Did he wonder that in his dream   Or was it after he awoke
The tale of warriors who looked toward their ideal
                                                and fell with a thud —
he had watched that with his wife on late-night television
Just the regimental colors alone
fluttered in the wind of a bewildered season
                                          near the bodies of the dead
He stirs the water inside the dirty cup
Telephone poles are lined up like chopsticks
and the bus scrapes past them
The man decides to go back to the rose garden again
because in dreams at least   one is supposed to be free
but instead what appeared was an exam hall
The terror of having the end approach
                                        when one is not prepared

Just as he was meditating that
this might be the time he should renounce the world
and become a monk
and match the gatekeeper in pressing for admission fees
the bus arrived at his transfer station
Just then the same flags he saw in his dream
droop this morning as there is no wind
and even the first bus of the day
approaches with the same colors
rocking heavily despite the hour
The long wall along the park continues to the top of the hill
Is his pursuer there
This course offers no place to hide
Inside the wall tall *keyaki* trees are sprouting new buds
The man sees all this from the corner of his eye
and realizes that spring certainly is a cruel season[10]
Buds swelling on trees in the city seems somehow unnatural
Cats falling in love also seems a bit forced
At the bottom of the hill a former village lies sunken
The man's legs go on tramping the morning dew
his body gradually rises up
Once there was a small factory here
bellows breathed fire
sweat dripped from the workers' bulging muscles
and a bamboo pipe mender would be blowing on his flute
or a wagon loaded with Chinese cabbage
would be standing outside
The child playing in the narrow street was the man's father
A dragonfly rests on the manual pump
in the communal wash area
and the woman chatting with neighbors was the man's mother
All that's left from those times is the temple
but its grounds have gotten much smaller
Over the scene of such memories

the man runs wearing a La Coste shirt
a little tired like the bus
but nevertheless wearing a smile
All he's interested in now is "family bliss"
He pays no attention to
cucumber blossoms growing by the well
    lipstick traces on the spring air
or to the yellow of forsythia
                gorgeous at the shabby kitchen door
or the rust at the propane gas cylinder cock
or automobile graveyards the glitter of mountains
                              of industrial waste
or urban planning or change of government
"And the rain fell upon the town
wetting the soft dry grass
rain that burgeons gardens to green"[11]
or
"The wind from time to time
became bells or spilled bush clover"
           poetic thoughts like these leave him cold
Come to think of it in the neighborhood the man
                                 is running through
no rain has fallen in a long time nor has wind blown
Until the other day the black hole of broken glass
seemed like a wicket looking onto the age
                          the old house on the corner
disappeared
and a self-service gasoline stand took its place
but it doesn't look like business is so good
It was around then that the white dog appeared
from nowhere in particular stoutly asserting his existence
Surely
rain softened the man's heart
the woman too grew gentler changed her doll's kimono

and pressed for flight to the castle and from the castle
"let's die together"   she babied up to him like that sometimes
The wooden boards of the kitchen floor
                                        his mother had polished crying
shone black   and threw back the voices of doves
                                                    singing in the eaves
in those days when soundlessly falling rain
fell continuously inside the heart also

The dog was used to people
He didn't stick out from the frame of time
much less try to run after the man

5

Up on the hill
the running man discovers
      not clouds   but a police box[12]
a cherry tree behind it
He would like to ask   not for some address
                                      but about the soul of Yamato[13]
but the blossoms aren't blooming yet
(Seeing how the policeman sleeps
maybe they never will
besides   this intersection gets so much exhaust
our ancestors must be disappointed)
the running man brings
                                    his ragged breathing under control
Feeling hungry   he heads for home
In the small yard   his two children are playing
the way they're pushing the swing so hard is dangerous
(Happiness breaks easily   so let's be careful)
the man slackens his pace

Seeing the vapor rising from his head
the children cry "Daddy's home" into the house
and look back to ask "Why do you run so much"
The man doesn't know either
But he can take comfort
in the feeling he still has of firmly holding the documents
because this above all he does not want to lose
"You'll understand when you grow up"
he answers without confidence
and feeling somehow relieved   he wipes away his sweat
At any rate he had come home all right
Many among his friends have died
(Guys with poor luck are hopeless)
he removes his chrysanthemum-stamped headband
A spindly cherry tree stands in his garden
but by this point it's pure formality
an abstract being
The man   standing still   realizes there's a rainbow
over his eyelashes
and is astonished
When did they settle in
the tribe of dragons
who make mirages by spitting out their spirits[14]
Emotion appears between the waves of air turbulence
A dappled shadow falls
and leaving behind the man wondering
was the neighborhood I just ran through an illusion
or was the reappearance of the sunken village an
illusion the rainbow soon dissolves
The idea of calling a mirage "city of the sea"[15]
without doubt was born of an intellect from a faraway age
in a faraway country
Realizing he hasn't seen the sea in awfully long
the man looks back on all the time he's spent running

He'd take the children clam-digging next vacation
remembering this he repeats his running steps
and gazes fondly upon the kids
Where did it come from   a white mongrel
one leg raised   is doing his business at the frail cherry tree
No   that's not his pursuer   the man heaves a sigh of relief
looks for the still undelivered documents
and realizes they're gone
Just as his heart begins to throb violently
his wife appears in the doorway
and calls brightly   "Breakfast is ready dear"

And from behind her a white dog
                    this time the real one
comes running   comes after him
pat pat pat   pat pat pat   pat pat
a little larger than before

---

1 Adam Smith, *The Wealth of Nations*: the words used to define the principle of self-regulation in the market.

2 Takayanagi Shigenobu's haiku "run, else we are all pampas grass" from his book of selected haiku, *Yamakawa Semio Kushu*.

3 Luke, Matthew.

4 Sung in "*Tohryanse*," a children's game like "London Bridge," where the children pass through a temple gate formed by joined and upraised hands.

5 The traditional garb of a Japanese wayfarer.

6 Proposed slogan for Mitsukoshi department store ads long ago.

7 Shinran (Buddhist monk, 1173-1262), "To say nothing of evil men," from *Tannishoh*.

8 Mahler, "The Song of the Earth"; original poem by Li Po.

9 The stadium where all-Japan high school baseball championships are held

every spring and summer. A Japanese institution, these games are televised nationwide and figure in the dreams of many a ball-playing boy.

10 T. S. Eliot, "The Waste Land."

11 Anonymous.

12 Suggested by the title of Shiba Ryohtaro's novel, *The Cloud on the Hill.*

13 Japan.

14 *Shinkiroh,* the Japanese word for 'mirage,' derives from the ancient belief that mirages were caused by giant clams exhaling their spirits.

15 *Kaishi*, another word for mirage.

Man Sitting

From the sitting man's brow
hangs a cloud
time melts and expands into afternoon light
the outlines of letters blur
and a red camellia falls with a soft plop
Leaves tremble and disappear into the fog
For a while the birds clamor
and after they all fly off together
a low constant sound from somewhere
like the chanting of sutras or an incantation
plunges the surroundings into grayness
and the man is peeled off bit by bit
In the seas of printed labels
  from the full-color world map
in the vague frontiers remaining
  from the future plans of neighborhoods
he can see the eye swimming
To continue living still
his body laid on the tip of the pier
          along which it had come running
looks for someone blowing a bugle
    So once again
    he has to take part in the ball game he thinks
    half in dread half in anticipation
      the bright bamboo grove seems distant
A figure in the middle of a heaving wave of people
sticking only his head out
and searching for an island in the sun

is reflected upon the man's withered heart
A hopeless rain comes falling softly
Through the diffused landscape
a transparent dog comes running
Like a shadow   as if with some purpose
The man opens his eyes wide in fright
lowers his left shoulder   and listens with his one good ear
trying to hear the dog's panting
Since its tongue is hanging from its mouth
there should be a smell of sweat   yet
everything is moving slowly
and the running figure   scanned closely
                                        seems to be swimming
Suddenly enveloped by some shapeless thing
he turns around   still seated
protesting the feeling that begins to waft behind him
he sees a man with his own face sitting there
Steadily the man looks this way
as if saying   "It's time to change places"
Hurriedly   looking for a chance to turn round again
the man lowers his right shoulder
When he finally faces forward in even greater confusion
(the surroundings are too quiet for a scene of secret strife)
one more flower   of red camellia falls
The color of blood ultimately unshed
it disappears in the fog

Man Standing in a Storm

The storm is howling
The sky begins painfully to speak
Treetops writhe   baring their anxiety
The man standing in the storm becomes small
and stooping over   peers into the birdhouse
Clouds tear into pieces and flee
As there is no war or revolution
he can't exactly tower over the flow
so   mindful of his heart   he excretes the smoke of sheep
The clouds' edges glitter
send rain down on a medieval world map
and make sunlight illuminate re-zoned neighborhoods
From within the odor of mold
a schooner departs in search of new islands
Silverfish leap   sketching the romance of the South Seas
The surroundings are gentler than usual
because boredom is eddying at the cyclone's eye
The man lifts his face and runs his gaze along the horizon
On his eyelids and cheeks   rain begins harshly to fall
The grass and the trees are like the unkind days
he cannot recall   songs he has forgotten
Oleander and althea are blooming
but Earth's wounds are too deep
          love could not save the planet
as he is thinking thus in past tense
ants   not on a pilgrimage to Kumano[1]
unfazed by the storm   come crawling out
                    of the turnstiles in droves

Monsters called Fleshies flood the scene
and amble around like an occupying army
Before he knows it they have entered the building
and they sit down behind the man
all wearing the same expression
quietly as if in pity as if to drive him away
It was around then that the wind grew stronger
The sun hid and the river stopped its murmur
This way he could better have peace of mind
So he hurled hydrangeas crocodile livers word processors
into the air
and frequented bars
The castle walls soar above the conquered swamp
covered with reeds of uncouth Dow-Jones averages
and flowers of the founder's family crest
The building rocks like a ship before it's wrecked
the man trying to sober up remains standing on the roof
Trying anew to survey the movement of the tides
he opens his eyes inside the storm
On the mast the pension-eagle rests his wings
The anchor is made of pure conception
and awaits being thrown into the swamp
If at that time thunder were to roll
the only thing the man could do would be to crouch low
With an air of sensing neither crisis nor tension
the wind pushes closer becoming countless layers
of flocks of sheep
The man braces his legs planting himself in place
and calls to mind the great deeds of distant ancestors
but at the sound of the PA system announcing
the end of the day
the fortress' form and the lonely castle walls disappear
and entering on the revolving stage

is a birdhouse covered in the vines of a weir
swaying in the storm its branches breaking
The man hunches his shoulders and goes inside the birdhouse
A rainbow that had failed to explode
grunts discontentedly and smashes into the door
The man's apron-clad wife comes running out
and claps her hands
"Oh, Daddy, I'm glad we have you"
Just then the wind grew in violence
and the sheep went running up into the sky

---

1 *"Ari no Kumano-mohde,"* or "The Ants' Kumano Pilgrimage," was a phrase coined to describe the crowds of people pilgrimaging to the mountain shrines of Kumano, their long processions resembling trails of ants as they made their way up the mountainside.

Man Who Left Something Behind

A clock ticks the seconds away
and street sounds amble through the room
Clouds flow over the white plates
washing away last night's dreams
Slowly reeling in the thread
toward the depths of commotion drenching his body
weightless occurrences
are strung to it one at a time
Awaiting him as always   a day called today
Unchanging calculations
Unchanging crowds
Even if there is a gate in an alley passed by
make a point of not entering it
If stopped by kindness
the empty husk remaining would likely be insect-shaped
A faintly bluish breeze blows through the gaps
between vitamin tablets
Peeking over   he sees young leaves
swaying in the garden next door
Words play without yet finding expression
Most likely the wounds have become butterflies and flown
away
To seek flowers
Avoiding the doubts that arise in his mind
he flips through the newspaper
(Not having an exit doesn't mean I have to die)
Civil rights   even though only half   are still civil rights
Even in a lidded jar

sky-beans grow
Even shadowy changes are proof that one is alive
There is no need to choose one's destination oneself
Everything is determined
and the main thing is not to become obsessed
Even if regret should swirl around what one leaves behind—
"Know thyself"
Morning in any town
has its very own smells and coincidences
and no one could ever possess them
But is it possible to return
sound to sound itself[1]
and color to nature
The cry of the man who jumped from a roof yesterday
the ambulance siren swiftly erased
There are sausages on the plate
the man eats them with mustard
Better to have some piquancy
The salad is a fresh green
the cut faces of the orange glisten with juice
His watch announces the hour of departure
its quiet tone of authority soothes the spirit
The man puts on his jacket   tightens his tie
and scanning the room to see if he's forgotten anything
he sees another man sitting in the chair
Elbows propped on the table
he seems to be thinking
Trying to address him the man realizes it is himself
and his mood is spoiled
The sound of empty cans rolling somewhere
canters off   light and faint
The pinwheel creaking
atop the carp streamer pole next door
the sound spreading to every corner of the room

and suddenly it's dark out
"Fair with some clouds and occasional rain"
Turning he finds the other man gone
The walls are damp and shadows move
He remembers stars falling in his dream last night
Fortunately there was no rainbow
Relieved   the man opens the door   locks it
and feigning good spirits descends the stairs
Important to get oneself into the rhythm
"Good morning   Did you sleep well?"
The concierge   plastic bucket in hand
greets him cheerfully
The man shakes himself once and starts walking

---

[1] John Cage

Mountain Lilies

The receding figure of the wind sways
passing on toward the mountain ridge
As I strain to hear the whispered joy
of the mountain stream so soon run dry
the curfew trumpet I heard while napping
in childhood dreams of soaring through the sky
begins to sound once more
upon the copperplate of memory

The setting sun's light floats around me
and like a scene from a film viewed long ago
clouds are dyed crimson
Beyond the mountains   land yet in light
unrolls through evening haze
or so I imagine
with all the doubt that lives in a promise
Twilight closes over the valley
but these mountain lilies have not set
as the wind moves past once more

What is it that bears up this valley as it sinks
Gentleness Or is it foolishness
Here in the dimness
as I make ready to find the way
pride   not yet willing to sleep
        lingers over the flowers
recalling festivals that once flared
            like hellfire

As the shades become steadily deeper
and the Earth grinds on into darkness
the mountain lilies' fragrance grows stronger

A People Aspiring to Wandering Priesthood

The season is May   the time is morning
Youth   now aged   aspiring to wandering priesthood
hangs a mirror of wind on a bough
Women   hair flying   become bees and dive into flowers
Ancient horsecarts   phantom armies
move with the sound of hand organs
There once was a tribe that declined into ritual
gazing at fire that danced faraway in the darkness
Harsh times when birds turned to stone   fish to sand
Many suns froze
and only the apple tree bore red fruit
Serpents surrounded the table in the grassy plain
and quick-witted people   avoiding conflict   dove into vines
In the sky   purple flowers blossomed
Sheep lay down in crimson spring water
and spoke to pearls crystallizing into ultramarine
The stars moved slowly
and the camera obscura of the rose
                    measures time from between ribs
A strong north-northwesterly wind   blue sky
This morning again   newspapers smelling of ink were
  distributed
Foaming on countless ripples
the world is wholly peaceful
If so   this blowing inside the body
may be the sound of beating wings   cranes dreaming of
  explosion
In a crowd they surge toward the horizon

seeking the land that has vanished like smoke
Not finding it they are relieved   and despairing
Once more they grow fond of hard times
The season is May   the time morning
all of their friends have become wandering priests

Person Passing

Where shall I go
After here   across the bridge

Not like the wind exactly
but I always meant to interchange
fire and water
light and wind
I'm not lying
But I was shy so pretended to play
reciting poetry and stuff

When I look back my footsteps pursue me
Red like demon-weed
gleaming blue like phosphorus

Sins born one after another in dark celestial houses
Constellations spread their legs
and watching them   I'm almost sucked in
Just a moment ago   a pair of Noah's arks
were swallowed into the black hole
How long has it been
since the moon of civilization set
The rotating Earth
apparently goes on tilting quietly
strangely   toward the bright pool

After here
where shall I go

My hometown has sunk on the other side of time
and the castle into the water
so neither harps nor wind chimes sound but
silence is kept not only by morphous things
Myriad hopes
promises I couldn't keep

When I die
will my regrets beget flowers like lilies of the valley
The people left behind
will likely see a beggar in the mirror of memory
sitting and eating flowers
picking them with trembling hands

By then
the distant sight of happy families will have nothing to do with me
and a wintry wind will be blowing in the sky
Just like it always did when I was alive
freezing the night
Will the stars flicker wordlessly
as if telling the whereabouts of the soul
The surroundings are dark
and maybe for that reason all the more gay

There were neither flocks of melody's woes
nor the caravan's fanfare trumpets

The birds formed row upon row
and flew off beyond the precipice
When the carriage which departed bearing corpses
scattered the flowers of a deserted station
one by one

the whispers of the women who gathered
        begin preparing for their return to heaven

I want to celebrate
at least the gaiety of death
    with a heavenly banquet
but festivals always crawl upon the ground
mingle with the smoke of supper and hang there
The leaders   trying to gather the far-flung hearts
repeat their attempts to hold a wicked feast
Passers-by lower the brims of their caps
with vague smiles on their lips
draw themselves up and swagger off
Left swinging behind
a sign for shaved ice
a red lantern with the word *sake*

After here
where shall I go

When I close my eyes
myriad familiar sights flash on and off
and skyrockets burst in brilliance
Petals of proudly blooming flowers also fade
and looking for death   which went off somewhere
the stars begin twinkling again
warning that they cannot possibly
light the way

Seagull

Loosed from its binding ropes
the anchor sank into the sea
Sending up spray as in Hiroshige
it disappeared instantly into the depths
The seagull watched in silence
a feeling of regret rising in his heart
A body that has survived is light
so must hurriedly acquire something heavy-seeming
a fortune an education a steel bridge
Leaving everything else with the wind
the seagull circles and recalls the past

He cannot fly to the past the way we trace history
so he ends up regarding all as it is
Away from gentleness
the seagull continues to fly
The sky is dark the only blue spot a portion of sea
a sacred place none can approach
so without fear of being bewitched
                    by an illusory liberated zone
he swivels his neck in search of food
Once aiming for the sun he beat his wings
forgetting his companions

A rusty keel creaks
a wrecked ship that lost its compass
the low hut is behind it fishing nets flutter
and unlit paper lanterns dangle

Sand flies up   thoughts become confused
Into the mysteriously opened hole of memory
                                        a sudden shower pours
Like rain falling on the street   no
with the vehemence of washing away regret
wings beating
The waves bare white fangs
The seagull suddenly
                        for no reason wanting to burst out laughing
looks out over the sea
A headland from when he was rocked in a dark cradle
long ago beneath the precipice of time
appears dim in the spray
He tries out his voice but it falls far short of song
                                        like an ill-humored cat
and is swept away at once by the wind
The blue of the sea and the imagined blue of the sky
                                              come chasing after him
their color slightly muddied   dark
The sails fill with misfortune
Neither the landscape nor the story is an ally any longer
so toward the spaces of reality that remain to him
still unable to find the anchor
the seagull flies on

Spider

To bear his fate
the spider crouches
eight eyes gleaming
as the bat clamors for eyes
the web is shaped like a star
even holding evening dew   the threads grow gentle
Here outspread is language
obsessions   desires   distilled
upon them softly   cheerfully   a shimmer falls
The knots glimmer bead by bead
The flute notes born at that moment
run quick away across a distant field
at dawn becoming clouds
Toward a valley of rising mist
memories of sorrow move
The spider floats through illusion
even going to meet the snow
The spider is wind
when pausing   a solid shadow
black mirror
once   desiring transformation
a writhing wound
before you know it   memory-corroding rust
Even though ugly in appearance
he describes dreams that are lovely
says the oleander's red color
One foolish   distant summer
was heard the sound of an unseen flower blooming

the lilac sent forth its fragrance
and greenery danced   rustling   toward the heavens
On the nights of such days
gazing at the fountain of an abandoned garden
the spider sucks the life-juice of a moth
The wretchedness of livelihood preying on soft flesh
Atoning for one's sins means merely painting them over
so before he knew it   become a favorite of his day
the spider thrives
His threads expand his territory
Facing head-on his fate
which clings no matter how he tries to fling it free
the hunter of the night sobs
voicelessly
His underbelly turns a deep red
painted the color of shame
and a pattern of undisguisable jealousy surfaces
Discontent has now become a virtue
Effort at self-control changes slowly into melody
The spider afraid of uttering a sound
copes by zealously spinning thread
laughing with scorn at his futile efforts
midnight   a wind rises
The moon hides itself
and darkness spreads   pregnant with ill omens
Scent wafted from somewhere
seems to be pollen of evening primrose
bearing a sense of the Earth revolving
A toad lodges himself beneath the web
in love with the cloud
Hating how the shape of night
          becomes a sketch expelling putrid breath
The spider begins to devour his web
trying to witness the end of the world

relinquishing his malicious scheme
The threads were perhaps tired spirits of the forest
or of discontent
As an innocent child will lie out of curiosity
the spider seduces prey through the radiance of language
wrapping them in dazzle   intoxicating them
it may have been only a trick
to change darkness into light
all the more impressive for being unconscious
Eventually once more   a tired and bracing dawn
will probably come   without a sound
Then all that remains
will be a droplet-covered star
will it be the tears   or the cast-off shell
of the spider   who has hidden himself as he wished
Because it contains no elements whatsoever
it cannot be analyzed by anyone

Spoon

What a spoon scoops up —
is that the will to live
or is it the shadow of tired time
that falls upon the wall
No steam rises from the spoon
A distorted face attempting a return to daily life
in the gleam of tarnished silver
holding the hopes of those losing hope
between departed past
and haggard future
appears an foreseen resentment
appears a rainbow evoked by the spoon
appear thousands of vows of love
appears the lean face of lonely self-love
Hunger beautifies the landscape
and desperation gilds betrayal
The coldness of the spoon   closed in soft lips
Horseflies lured from the stable by foul breath
dance with a willful buzz
And   direct in its blindness
the pulse of independence
descends the thin tube toward darkness
when the weight of history's flotsam
awakens a faint breeze
The tongue becomes a dull harpoon
piercing the heap of dirty sediment
The spoon becomes the sharpened tip of augury
and searches out the language of pigs

In the sorrow of foolishness
and well-seasoned cunning
no longer knowing what it hopes for
habit moves the spoon
Apparently contented   the plump wrist
its hairy fingers eating the self's insides
stirs up the light on the plate
and sniffs with satiation
sounds of distant loneliness are heard
A rainbow when it disappears has definite mass

Telephone

Dialing a number
signifies surrender   sometimes
my finger even trembles in supplication
And there are moments
when the hand holding the receiver
stiffens in resentment
and my lips freeze   at the too-heavy blow
But the telephone has nothing to do with joy and sorrow
All we can say for certain
is that beyond this small machine glitter colored lights
an enormous city expanding for miles
Human will   replaced by zero through nine
crosses a crystal-like   steel-like sky
and runs through dark underground
Automatic switchboards are the knots in the net
Boastful bearers of a civilization
overripening with accumulated terror
run around
Night after day
they faithfully turn
senselessly creeping relationships   into movement
never even thinking of rest
When the telephone sits and waits
the sound of the wall clock ticking away the seconds
and the smell of fish grilling in the kitchen   both disappear
and the roar of the sea
and the creaking of commuter train couplings
can't be conveyed either

All conversation is made inorganic
by this crystallization of function
Inside a device feigning permanent neutrality
the exchange of love twisted with calculation
and the dark stream of humanity flowing in the streets
are both mediated by the oscillations of an integrated circuit
so simmering the receiver in a stone pot
will not extract its harshness
because it has no superfluous parts
like a ham bone   you won't find marrow that
melts in hot water
Soft flower petals that once flowed out of our ears
rainbow colors of hopes borne by the jellyfish
that walked from words
heart shapes that flew about
are now just yellowed documents of the past
The folly of fossil-loving nostalgia
Exposed ears   exposed mouths
make information flood out like auto-intoxication
so feeling hesitates like a submerged reef
in the black lump of the terminal
Even so   one day   like a subterranean stem
will the telephone communicate a furtive wish for
independence
One night
will it start ringing
To convey the point of the soul's emperor's argument
receiver becoming the hooves of the swan's knight
rapping on the doors of homes in a blockaded age
and gaining the ears of secretaries-general at countless
frontiers
On that day the city will be bathed in sunlight
like jungle treetops

and then the telephone will take its place
beside the sickle the pitcher the candlestick
not as the bailiff of the inorganic king but as a tool
For that to happen
the hand that holds the receiver now
must strike the ear to which it is held
Reject the messenger from civilization
and send forth a messenger to civilization
turn the long night
not into shuddering with fear of intrusion
but into silence preparing for attack
and splitting open not the enemy's white forehead
but your own
envelop the *objet* of function
Illusion is the last hope remaining
and treachery is a gamble trembling with reversal

Violets[1]

Let us cease to call affecting
a flower that concentrates surging emotion
into one color of bloom
That this purple deepened
by enduring the transformations around it
appears fascinating
is the pathos of spring
the shame of being alive
So whether criticized for pride
or accused of a lie
finding no words of reply
it merely smiles
And yet because it knows not why
it must imbed sharp rivets
into the landscape
the violet hangs its head as if to hide in the grass
and sees off sinners in straw hats
recalling a group of samurai that departed long long ago
  running
heroes defeated in battle who turned into butterflies
or the backs of Tartars crossing the sea
Unrealized hopes
they carried them all away
All that remains is gently sloping hills
and in the orchards a sense of peach blossoms falling
The sky wrapped in a thin veil
heightens with the singing of larks
The violet's crime has no name

Just an empty window opens onto the plain
and while a new traveler stops
to behold the sight
of the present being sucked into
the depths of antiquity
finding it somehow graceful
the grime of years creeps from his pores
and   wings flapping   flocks to the flowers
Just as he realizes
that the hunched figure wandering
in the depths of the tunnel of excavated time
is the child he left behind
the surroundings abruptly turn dark
spring   a dream within a dream
The jostling figures of individual lives appear
Birds' eggs, harmonicas, flags intermingle
and despite the commotion of the scene
not a sound can be heard
That the past   without reason
seems a sparkling wave
the flower's aura is to blame
or is it the weakness of a spirit weary from travel
As he lingers with the wish to have been born a small
  creature[2]
the new traveler's clothes   unnoticed   also are torn
the very image of a defeated samurai straggler
Here and there   violet blossoms emerge
and the tattered rags are truly the brocade of spring
When the madness eventually subsides
the surroundings are in prehistoric brightness
and the whisper of new leaves sprouting
for the first time   can be heard from afar

---

[1] Long ago, a traveler walking along a road turned back, and spent the day in a field.

There he found a bird's egg in the grass, which he put into his sleeve. Making himself a pillow of grass, he spent the night in the field, and there he had a dream: The egg was his child in a former life, and he must bury it in the field. When he awoke, the man did as his dream had instructed. Then, as he watched, a plant with one leaf sprouted, giving bloom to a purple flower. This was the plant we now know as the violet. (From Ancient Tales of the Fields.)

2 "Had I been born as small as a violet" — Natsume Soseki

Woman Singing

The singing woman moves upstream on the river of night
her voice her oar   she sweeps away time
Twisting her body she shoots her eyes upwards aslant
No stars are to be seen
the sound of the wind has died
The water splashes noise
and around her dress   artificial light clamors
The town's shadows sway
Rows of listening houses
crouch over hearths she left behind
Even if she laments her captivity
she doesn't know what holds her
so remembering young girls in chorus
or the sound of a dog howling at the moon
will not free her
Inevitably   a song sparkles inside her
and raises fireworks into the darkness
The flow of the river is gentle
and hackneyed phrases   newspaper articles
slowly   without rest   drift toward the sea
For whom was the banquet prepared
Only for those who cannot belong
Knowing she is permitted her song
the woman clasps her hands
and once more raises her voice
Like birds of passage that fly into a beacon lamp and fall
the melody hits a wall and scatters flower petals
The broken musical scales flutter lightly

and fly away into the night sky
In the path of dreams where she is left behind
the woman becomes burnt-out ashes

Woman Printing

Each day I print
I print myself
my shadow

At street-corner signals   greengrocer storefronts
bank counters and train stations
in the dreaming sky   the wind becomes streaks
Going North   tending South
they keep blowing   even inside my body
and tire me out
Returning home
it's not quite the same as usual
I look around the hushed room
The thermometer on the pillar
turns a red ill-humored eye
the light bulb swings its body and laughs
I was frightened and went outside

Studying the addresses in the neighborhood
this isn't no. 1 or no. 2
no. 3 and no. 4 are missing
is this an alley   Or should I say side street
Unfamiliar holes here

(This must be the dwelling place
of the imaginary numbers I studied long ago at school)
Nodding to myself   I enter
The window   its frosted glass like fog   is closed

from inside   steadily gazing this way are
my own eyes
Hurriedly I retreat   lie down on the sofa
at last feel myself come back to myself
My shadow   lost through too much printing
seems to have returned
I close my eyes in relief
a sandy beach opens
where waves of time pound upon my indecision
My small figure shows its back and walks away
I hear a sound that corrodes my insides
like the buzzing of horseflies
or the drone of a phone off the hook
< < < < < < < < < < < < < < < < < <

There is yet time in the late afternoon
So (that's not him)   I turn over
is it light or dark
In the diffused afterglow
three-cornered hats and paper whistles
exploded crackers, their streamers hanging
and the *hishimochi* and lanterns of the Doll Festival
are floating
Memories of drifting from elementary school
to a girls' high school
dress themselves up and gather   and dance
Restraining the desire to lean against my duplicate
I think of seeking my self as I will be
but am listless
and the noises of town resound like the roar of waves
In an effort to get deeper into reality
I curl myself up
and become a waterbug
a flea   a *magatama*

I lose rhythm
blend before long with the murky light

A bustling sound approaches
someone come riding a broom
or maybe the coach of Prince Charming
As I perk up only my ears
he passes my front door
(After all it's too soon for me to be called for)
Realizing he's entered another house I relax
roll up a yawn and toss it away
It becomes a hare
"Good evening it is time for you to get dressed"
I rise with annoyance
(I still had some printing to do)
ignoring that shadows have begun to dance
in the room now darker than before
I comb my hair put on a brassiere
(and notice that my nail polish is chipped)
I'll feel better when I put on some make-up
I apply some foundation stick out my tongue
wondering what painted face becomes me most
"Hey there"
says a voice
I turn my earrings jangling
My duplicate has quietly appeared and is seated near me
so vivid you couldn't tell which is the original
Come to this, I have no choice but to dance with my shadow
so I stand up pose coquettishly and dance a step
A flood of sound permeates every corner of my body
caresses me gently
but I see no form
I see my shadow softly take leave once again

Woman Wandering

Silent town
Everyone's gone away somewhere
In empty rooms dolls with eyes open as always
hold press conferences
and read Sherlock Holmes
Clocks sound the hours of absence
Water left boiling spilled over and wet the floor
made a faint stain and evaporated
There are no trees to shade the brilliant rays
of sun burning onto the pavement
The walls bake as well
fragments of quartz dazzle with reflected light
and here too no sign of human life
Rows of buildings on vacation
repulse the approach of crowds and become sanctuaries
Something is softly crawling behind them
Persistent as a thieving cat
it clings like a gecko
stands guarded hostile to the light
Though its outline is needlessly clear
its will may be all that moves
Blooming red a phantom flower
Within the water lily's noonday dream
floats a large black butterfly bereft of gravity
Invisible ash comes soundlessly drifting down
The woman is aging
Though still young her hands and face are etched with
  wrinkles
slowly advancing more slowly even than time

When she looks up at the sky
as if trying to swallow the town
the rising thunderclouds glitter at their edges
and sound the legendary lute
The woman wanders   seeking the wind
of a former time   when there were brave men
of a time when women knitted in the shade of a tree   and wept
Drops of coal tar trickle onto computers
and porcelain drums tremble at the brink of madness
but squalls and wind are both ancient tales
The woman is rich
possibly even richer than the gold beetle
Her bankbook   enmeshed   continues its self-propagation
While she contributed to the GNP
faraway countries were flooded
Deserts echoed with gunfire
In Africa   locusts devoured whole forests
The towns have no history
so escalators bearing no one
climb silently up to the sky
making a creaking sound no one can hear
Sensing an atmospheric pressure change the woman stirs
and looks back without a sound
She stretches her arm and tries to grasp
the way the sound of roadside trees rustling in unison
resembles a choir bemoaning the dead
her fingers bent
as if trying to grasp death
Failing   she turns her head
and laughs   mouth splitting from ear to ear

Woman Writing in Her Journal

The woman bites her nails
Becoming in her mind the characters
unconsciously she chews her pen
            the clothes they were wearing
            the voice of the man who spoke to her
she responds
with the concentration of craft
Lit by the brilliance of her teeth
the room's interior begins to crystallize
and in the mirror an infant appears
Crawling it comes closer
as though moving until the edge of time
The one who was standing in her dream last night
resembled the child she had washed away
As she gazes upon the infant hoping this one too should fall
it raises its head laughs
and fires a pistol
The smoke swirls to a small madness
a chorus of singing bursts forth
Rising to the sky it becomes an arabesque
The star-shaped designs all twinkle at once and are caught
  in the net
tremble here and there take on the shapes of birds
Fluffy clouds of drowsiness surge
solve geometry
and erase grammar
The woman rests her writing hand
brushes away a strand of hair with a little finger

and bares her ear to be caressed
From the expanding silence
faint rustling sounds
come gathering round her lovely self
People who have died   the whisper of passed hours
the voices of creatures wriggling inside the soil
or is it the sound of the blood that flows within her
As she sits thinking   head to one side
she even begins to feel perhaps she was born at the edge of
  the sea
where a bankless river flows in
a ruined boat lies on its side
waves splash against it even now
Her feeling of forsakenness grows
A fountain of sorrow springs from her journal
curves a gentle arc and envelops her
In the wish to call forth a new life for herself
she studies her face in the mirror
Sees herself falling with legs spread
Her breath   struggling up and ceasing
is stained purple and yellow
and seems to go under the waves   again and again
At the embrace   the room turns dark
Running at the depths adjacent to death
the woman tries to escape   resisting
to feel it even more deeply
As she stretches her hand toward a bird that has flown
her ring glints and becomes a grace note
Flying   flying   and looking back
she sees the egg breaking   a violet flower blooming
and under the aimless clouds
a lonely haunted mansion standing
She walks toward it   thinking what's this
and finds a white cloth

It has the shape of a person
so pleasure may be dancing there
        Where has the bliss of being violated gone
        I was holding hands with the joy of betrayal
        yet nothing has happened all day today
Giving up   the woman closes her journal   and stands
Suddenly   wanting to mount a horse
and gallop clear through town

Reflections

Editor, Thomas Fitzsimmons

The Colors of Poetry: Essays on Classic Japanese Verse by Ooka Makoto

Haiku: Messages from Matsuyama by Yagi Kametaro

A Poet's Anthology: The Range of Japanese Poetry by Ooka Makoto

Water Ground Stone, by Thomas Fitzsimmons and Karen Hargreaves-Fitzsimmons

Stages and Views, by Penny Harter